REMINDER

Poems and Photographs by

P.B. LUBEGA

Published by

PALU Enterprises, LLC

Rockville, Maryland 20852

2015

ISBN-978-0-9862322-0-6

Copyright © by Patricia Lubega 2014

All Rights Reserved. No part of this book may be reproduced or transmitted in any form or by any means without written permission from the author.

CONTENTS

DEDICATION 6

INTRODUCTION 7

REMINDER 8

HOW DO I LOVE YOU 24

PARENTS-EYE-VIEW... 26

YOU'RE ALWAYS THERE 28

YOUR TEARS... 32

MOM'S LOVE APPRECIATED 34

AWESOME LOVE 36

MOM I AM.. 38

I SAT ALONE IN SUMMER 40

MAKE HAY 42

ABOUT THE AUTHOR... 44

In honor
of the wonderful soul I met at birth

BERNICE LAURA GRAVES GILL FRALEY

She has taught me the meaning of
faith
She has shown me the importance of
hope
She has blessed me with the greatest gift
of all
-LOVE-
and

God has blessed my entire life with her

INTRODUCTION

Most of the poems in this book have been written throughout the years. Some have been presented as tributes on various holidays and others when an incident, object or thought has become a catalyst for inspiration.

The poem that represents the name of this work is one of the more recent and was born out of an effort to come to terms with the idea that the day might come when I would find myself on this earth and not be able to see or speak to my mom.

Several months after we celebrated Mom's ninetieth birthday, she started experiencing blackouts, falls, dramatic weight loss, memory loss, and general disorientation; I began to think that, perhaps, I should prepare for any eventuality and, although she has improved and is doing well, the concern still lingers.

Mom has always been spiritual, generous, and progressive. She has not only supported me throughout my life, but has cared for many others as well. Therefore, it was very important to find a way to express my deep love and appreciation for her. I felt that this tribute should be tangible, unique and current.

With all of this in my heart, I stepped outside and saw the little yellow rosebud depicting all that I wanted to convey. Its existence was indicative of the magnificence and glory within which we all live. Its story is the story of each of us. Its truth is the universal truth.

These photographs and poems, small examples of the myriad of blessings we receive constantly, are meant as a 'Reminder', not only to Mom but to all who see them, that God always has and always will hold us in the palm of His hand.

REMINDER

A tiny yellow rosebud
Unfurled its leaves one day
Peeked out upon a world of sticks
Dead leaves and decay

Beside it a toppled pot
In which a plant had stood
That now lay on the ground
Amidst the dirty wood

So all who ventured out
On that dismal autumn morn
Just had to stop and stare
To see perfection born

In the middle of depression
When it seemed the sun was lost
A reminder of redemption
Without a single cost

The little yellow rosebud
With tears of sparkling dew
Reflected those in my own eyes
As I lovingly thought of you

For when all is said and done
And burdens fall at last
The spirit of joy is what remains
And in our hearts is cast

As autumn days grew shorter
And winds blew strong and cold
The lovely little rosebud stood
Determined, straight, and bold

It's pretty shade of yellow
Took on a deeper hue
As if of golden honey
As from bud to bloom it grew

And those to whom this gift
Was granted daily, in awe,
Still paused and wondered
That the rose had not a flaw

Petals pointing toward heaven
Reaching out as if in prayer
Not beseeching, not entreating
But poised and praising there

No fancy speeches given
No proposal or accolade
No special supplication
Or bargain of deals made

For in the keeping of nature
The realization of a legacy
Requires only attention
To our Creator's majesty

The time for flowering buds
Had already come and gone
But the chosen work for one
Having started, lingered on

For the rose's petal arms
In extending its affections
Had opened its blossoms
To reach in all directions

And those who passed by
Enjoying sight and smell
Went on with joyful hearts
And grateful souls as well

Smiling bright, stepping light
Men of power, trash, and mail
Happy voices, smiling faces
Kids and women on the trail

No one knew just what it was
But they all felt energized
Loving, caring, gladly sharing
Each a miracle in disguise

Graces won by acts of praising
So steeped in deep devotion
That they fill earth and beyond
With no banter or commotion

And at her mission's end
Rose's petals paled in hue
Still beautiful but different
Embracing the evening dew

A canopy of holly berries
All shiny green and red
Serving as was its destiny
To back the manger bed

With his parents watching
A babe in straw did lie
Angel neighbors caroling
With love were passing by

A carefully woven spider web
As a star might have been
Reflecting light from the moon
Enhanced this blessed scene

Without thought for the past
Or what was yet to come
Amidst the joy of love and peace
Relaxed, rose did succumb

Into earth's majestic arms
So lovingly awaiting
Each cherished petal held
By God officiating

How do I love you? There are no ways to count
In a myriad inconceivable, defying an amount
For all the stars in the sky or fish in the deep blue sea
Cannot begin to compare to what you mean to me

Where do I love you? Why I do in every place
In every nook and cranny; there is no hidden space
Where you are not present; beyond all thought and sight
Deep in my heart and soul where there's no day or night

When do I love you? For now and always, it's true.
There really is no time when my heart is not with you
When life is good and peaceful and even when it's sad
When I'm feeling at my peak and when I'm feeling bad

Why do I love you? I know but can't explain
You tear away my baggage and rip apart my pain
Hug me with your kindness whenever there's a trial
Elevate and surround me with your glowing smile

How do I love you? It's too difficult to tell
For just a thought of you makes my spirit swell
An eternal gift of love and joy in every circumstance
Is what you are, My Love, and it's definitely not by chance!

PARENTS-EYE-VIEW

High atop a mountain of anxiety
Amidst clouds of doubt and fear
Parents regard their offspring
Pretending to disappear

Clearing skies improve their vision
As they hover over their dear
Ones trying diverse ways
Of thinking, doing then moving on

Sunshine bursts with brilliant splendor
Illuminating each glistening tear
And shining on each budding novice
Advancing to complete the sphere

Of understanding and truth in
Undulating torrents of love from year to year
Ancestors to descendants and back
Forever timeless yet moving on

Through fogs of uncertainty
And dark clouds of fear

Through thunders of impulse
And jolts of reality that sear

Through pounding repercussions
And unrelenting trials

Through storms of bleak delusion
And rivers of denials

Through hurricanes of refuse
And tornados of trash and lies

Through cyclones of anxiety
And a deluge of woeful cries

Through glistening rain of tears
And pain as piercing spears

YOU MOM YOU!

Through rainbows of commitment
And bouquets of selfless giving

Through daybreak's beam of hope
And sunlight's smile on living

Through bright rays of laughter
With your caring shove

Through deep forests of stillness
And breezes bearing love

Through showers of unsought blessings
And grateful lakes of charity

Through the evening song of prayer
And gifts of joy and clarity

Through life's unending party
With love that's strong and hearty

YOU MOM YOU!

My heart is drenched by your tears
Laden with the frugality
Of apprehension ignited by fears
That your sense of reality
Might, one day, seem as wasted years

So linger not in the muck and mire
Of misunderstanding
Nor wallow in the ego's flagrant ire
For, more outstanding
Is the joy that love will always inspire

My heart rests on the horizon of hope
As sure as the sun is rising
And a rainbow announces the scope
Of how the compromising
That fills its gold pot helps us to cope

For the blessed gift of connection
Radiating from our Source
Overcomes feelings of rejection
And is a miraculous force
That assures our hearts' protection

Beyond the morning hours that start with baths and showers
Through the oils and pressings before donning our dressings
Even when you brush our hair or raise the window to let in air
We know your loving care is driven and by a Godly spirit given

Fighting our battles every day and nurturing us along the way
Smiles and kisses all around lift us as we're outward bound
In your love we see perfection far beyond our hearts' reflection
Soaring high as butterflies' wings, it is the loveliest of all things!

Awesome love
Does not hesitate; it participates
Does not ask, "What can I do?" or
"Do you need help?"
It does not say, "If you need me call me."
Does not come with 'ifs', 'ands' or 'buts'
It does not make 'token' gestures.
No excuses. No explanations.
It just jumps right in.
It is already there and already working.
It can never be reciprocated
It does not count scores.
It shows up on time all the time.
No questions asked. No holds barred.
It makes no promises. It imposes no conditions.
Have you ever been a recipient of awesome love?
Have you ever loved awesomely?
It is nice to be loved awesomely but
It is Divine to love awesomely!

MOM I AM

Your spirit soaring

Your smile adoring

Your emotions searing

Your eyes tearing

Your forward vision

Every brave decision

Your brow sweating

Your cares fretting

Your nerves fraying

Your lips praying

Mom I am your heart beating

MOM YOU ARE

My bell ringing

My voice singing

My goals' hoping

My life coping

My deeds inspiring

Every plan aspiring

My darkness lighting

My hand writing

My sight seeing

My soul being

Mom You are my heart beating

I sat alone in summer's warmth
Hugged by a comforter of peace.
An honor guard of stately trees
Confidently stationed before me
Unwittingly revealing their truth
Of years of unconditional service
Sheltering, comforting, inspiring
A gentle breeze stirred from afar
Then advanced slowly and gingerly
As if seeking each giant's approval
To convey a reality as old as time.
Gently, it wrapped itself around me
And tenderly caressed my face.
I felt its loving and eternal vow
"You are my heart's perfection
Enthralled by you, I cannot turn
I am yours always and forever."

MAKE HAY

It may seem as if time is flying
So much has been said and done
Drastic change there's no denying
Has affected nearly everyone

But getting down to the nitty-gritty
The core of all things is the same
Service that's loving, jovial and witty
Is a gift only a few can claim

If few are chosen from the many called
Where does that put you, My Love?
Why far beyond the slow and the stalled
You are lifetimes and eons above!

Now when all has been said and done
As I've already made very clear,
The only thing left is to honor this pun
"Make hay while the sun shines!" My Dear!

Shortest and longest reigning family members

Aden Shane Yiga Lubega (August 26, 2014)

and great grandmother

Bernice Laura Graves Gill Fraley (February 10, 1923)

ABOUT THE AUTHOR

P.B. Lubega, mother of six and grandmother of nine, has led an illustrious life that has included farming, diplomacy and many projects in between. Born in Detroit MI in 1940, to very young parents, she is a graduate of Wayne State University with a degree in Sociology and is Master educated in Elementary Education.

She left Detroit in early 1964 to fly to Uganda, East Africa, the home of her husband, diplomat, Mathias K.L. Lubega and has had the privilege of living in a number of countries which also include Ghana, Russia, Ethiopia, and Kenya.

Seeking ways to enhance community development, education and international cooperation at every available opportunity, her efforts have resulted in the establishment of several organizations including The African Women's Association in Addis Ababa, Ethiopia which sent a delegation to the United Nations Organization for International Women's Day. She has been honored in the U.S.A. and Uganda for her contributions to education.

On a personal level, Gramma Pat, as she is affectionately called by some, loves music and has held starring roles as Cassilda in Gilbert and Sullivan's 'The Gondoliers', The Fairy Godmother in James Marshall's version of 'Cinderella' and many other productions as a member of The English Dramatic Society in Ethiopia.

She has staged productions for Uganda Television and produced a three act play, Snow White and the Seven Dwarves at the Uganda National Theater which led to her having been invited to serve on its Board of Directors.

Due to political unrest in Uganda, she returned to Detroit, taught for ten years and established "BEAM Drama Club" (Best Entertainment Around Motown) giving young people an opportunity to experience freedom of expression through singing, dancing and acting.

She now spends most of her time working with young people, writing and making beaded jewelry and greeting cards which she sells to help fund Ka's Kid's Educational Fund in honor of her son, Kaggwa Lubega. She has a number of other works soon to be published.

www.ingramcontent.com/pod-product-compliance
Lightning Source LLC
Chambersburg PA
CBHW041755040426
42446CB00001B/44